ARTIFICIAL INTELLIGENCE

STEM: SHAPING THE FUTURE

ARTIFICIAL INTELLIGENCE

COMPUTING AND THE INTERNET

GENETIC ENGINEERING

MEDICAL DISCOVERIES

ARTIFICIAL INTELLIGENCE

DAVE BOND

MASON CREST

Mason Crest
450 Parkway Drive, Suite D
Broomall, Pennsylvania 19008
(866) MCP-BOOK (toll free)

©2017 by Mason Crest, an imprint of National Highlights, Inc.
Printed and bound in the United States of America.
CPSIA Compliance Information: Batch #STFM2017.
For further information, contact Mason Crest at 1-866-MCP-Book.

First printing
1 3 5 7 9 8 6 4 2

on file at the Library of Congress
    ISBN: 978-1-4222-3710-6 (series)
    ISBN: 978-1-4222-3711-3 (hc)
    ISBN: 978-1-4222-8073-7 (ebook)

QR CODES AND LINKS TO THIRD-PARTY CONTENT

TABLE OF CONTENTS

KEY ICONS TO LOOK FOR:

Words to understand: These words with their easy-to-understand definitions will increase the reader's understanding of the text while building vocabulary skills.

Sidebars: This boxed material within the main text allows readers to build knowledge, gain insights, explore possibilities, and broaden their perspectives by weaving together additional information to provide realistic and holistic perspectives.

Educational Videos: Readers can view videos by scanning our QR codes, providing them with additional educational content to supplement the text. Examples include news coverage, moments in history, speeches, iconic sports moments and much more!

Text-dependent questions: These questions send the reader back to the text for more careful attention to the evidence presented there.

Research projects: Readers are pointed toward areas of further inquiry connected to each chapter. Suggestions are provided for projects that encourage deeper research and analysis.

Series glossary of key terms: This back-of-the book glossary contains terminology used throughout this series. Words found here increase the reader's ability to read and comprehend higher-level books and articles in this field.

WORDS TO UNDERSTAND

artificial intelligence (AI)—a branch of computer science dealing with the simulation of intelligent behavior in computers

artificial neural network (ANN)—a computing system made up of a number of simple, highly interconnected input and output processing elements, in which information that flows through the network affects its structure because the network changes— or learns, in a sense—based on that input and output

intelligence—the ability to learn, understand, or deal with new or trying situations

intelligence quotient (IQ)—a number used to express the apparent relative intelligence of a person based on a standardized test

Moore's law—a principle of microprocessor development usually holding that processing power doubles about every 18 months, especially relative to cost or size

Turing test—a proposed test of a computer's ability to think, requiring that the hidden substitution of the computer for one of the participants in a keyboard and screen dialogue should be undetectable by the remaining human participant

CHAPTER 1

INTRODUCTION TO ARTIFICIAL INTELLIGENCE

MANY PEOPLE UNDERSTAND *intelligence* to be the ability to learn, understand, or deal with new or trying situations. But what do we really mean by intelligence? Can we measure it? Is it something we develop, or are we simply born with it? Can we create intelligence in another entity such as a machine?

A lawyer can use a computer database to access details about every court case ever recorded. The machine holds more information than the lawyer's memory can, but so far only a human has the imagination to use the knowledge effectively.

ARTIFICIAL INTELLIGENCE DEFINED

Artificial intelligence (AI) is a branch of computer science dealing with the simulation of intelligent behavior in computers. It moves toward creating machines that are "intelligent"—that can think for themselves, communicate, and act in some of the same ways as humans. Truly intelligent machines that think as independently and broadly as humans do not yet exist, but scientists are busy working to develop this new generation of computers with a great deal of money invested in the research.

In this book, we will look at progress in AI research and consider some of the questions this new technology raises. There are many complex issues about how far AI technology should go and whether the benefits will outweigh the possible problems. The more people are informed on these topics, the better society can navigate a world with emerging AI in the future.

This book will not prescribe how you should think about AI. Instead, it will provide historical, technical, and social background on the field and bring to light different views and future implications. Then you can form your own opinions and discuss the issues from an informed perspective, engaging the topic of AI in a meaningful way.

CONCEPTS OF INTELLIGENCE

In order to make sense of AI, we need to understand what intelligence is. Exams often test knowledge and memory rather than intelligence. A computer could be programmed to do well on exams, but would that make it intelligent? While there are many variations on the definition of intelligence, common components include the following:

- Learning new concepts from different sources, including experiences
- Understanding and applying information to manipulate one's environment
- Solving problems in new or trying situations
- Anticipating the consequences of events and actions

Other factors may include consciousness, awareness of other people, and a sense of morality. So how can we create all this in a computer, and what has been done thus far?

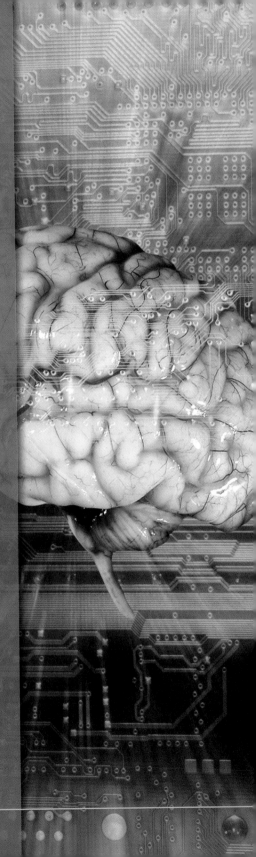

 **SIDEBAR**

CONSCIOUS COMPOSER

"Not until a machine can write a sonnet or compose a concerto because of thoughts and emotions felt... could we agree that machine equals brain—that is, not only write it, but know that it had written it."

—*Sir Geoffrey Jefferson, Professor of Neural Surgery, Manchester University, 1949*

HISTORY OF AI

AI is a concept that dates all the way back to ancient times. Jewish legends of the golem conceived of an automated servant that was made from clay and could be brought to life by placing a magic token in its mouth. Removing the token would return the golem to unanimated clay. The idea of intelligent robots was also found in the Greek myths of Hephaestus, a blacksmith who manufactured mechanical servants, and the bronze man, Talos.

In the 13th century, Albert Magnus and Roger Beacon created the first human head models that could talk. Leonardo da Vinci made a walking lion in 1515—as clockmakers started using their skills to create mechanical animals—and in the early 17th century, Rene Decartes proposed that the bodies of animals were merely complex machines.

Blaise Pascal created the first mechanical digital calculating machine in 1642. In 1801, Joseph Marie Jacquard invented the Jacquard loom, the first programmable machine, with instructions on punched cards. Seventeen years later, Mary Shelley published *Frankenstein*, about a young scientist who creates an independently conscious creature. In 1936, Alan Turing proposed the universal Turing machine, the origin of the first digital computer. He then created a test in 1950 to determine intelligent behavior in machines.

Modern history in AI begins with the stored-program computer, invented by John von Neumann in 1953. In 1956, John McCarthy coined the term "artificial intelligence" at the Dartmouth Conference. The same year, Allen Newell, J.C. Shaw, and Herbert Simon developed the first AI computer program, the Logic Theorist. From 1974–1980, criticism on investments in AI and pressure from Congress led to reduced government funding in the United States (US) and United Kingdom (UK), known as the "AI winter." This was reversed in the 1980s when the UK increased funding in AI to compete with Japanese efforts.

In 1997, IBM's Deep Blue became the first computer to defeat a chess champion when it won against grandmaster Gary Kasparov. In 2005 and 2007, respectively, robots drove 131 miles on a new desert trail and successfully navigated 55 miles of an urban environment while following traffic laws. The answering system Watson won the quiz show Jeopardy in 2011, competing against former champions Brad Rutter and Ken Jennings.

In 2014, Eugene Goostman developed a chatbot, a computer program that simulates human conversation with people over the Internet. It convinced one-third of test judges that it was a human being responding in dialogue, though this was partly due to its claim that it was an adolescent that spoke English as a second language.

AI RESEARCH WITH A PURPOSE

Leading the research into AI is the Massachusetts Institute of

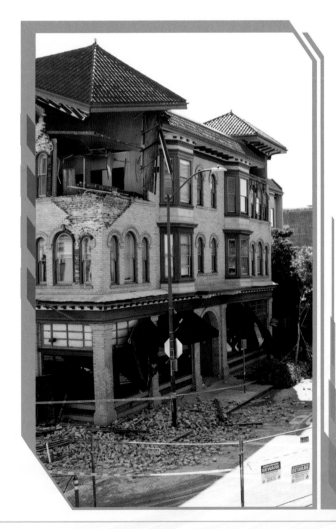

The potential for AI is particularly great in rescue work. Places like this earthquake-damaged building in California may be too dangerous for humans to work in.

Technology (MIT). Scientists there have developed machines that can learn, see, talk, and move around sensibly by learning where obstacles are and avoiding them. The scientists' work is not only for research but also with practical intentions in mind. They hope that by better understanding AI, they will be able to build computers and machines with a wide range of useful functions.

Because there are many potential uses for AI, scientists aim to develop different systems for targeted functions. Already, we are seeing advanced software that can work with huge amounts of data to reach intelligent conclusions. This can be done on computers that look no different from those we use every day. We have robots that look mechanical but can move independently and get information from their surroundings by seeing, touching, and hearing in ways similar to humans. Currently, there is rapid progress in developing "living" robots that look, talk, move, and act just like we do.

A computer can "know" more than a human can in terms of sheer storage of information. It can deal with many facts at once, comparing details and making judgements more quickly and thoroughly than we can. There are already computer systems that use specialized knowledge to solve problems, the most advanced of which are called expert systems. A medical expert system

French mathematician Blaise Pascal invented one of the first mathematical calculating machines during the seventeenth century.

might play the part of a doctor, able to quickly compare a patient's symptoms and medical history with a huge database of illnesses.

FUNCTION VS. FASHION

Many AI systems—often called AIs—look nothing like living beings because doing so might be less advantageous for them. Some AI robots have wheels or other special tools that are more effective than human features for performing certain tasks. But some AIs may be built to look like people or animals for social functions. We would react very differently to an AI being that looked like a person rather than, say, a refrigerator.

This UNIVAC computer from the mid-1950s took up most of a large room. It was one of the first computers capable of storing program instruction in its electronic memory.

You might think it would be great to have a robot to organize your closet and make your tea. But would a robot ever give you unhealthy food like potato chips or accept that your outfit is more trendy when it is untucked and messy looking? This would need a human touch. So far computers have difficulty taking into account factors they have not been "taught" or told how to deal with, but to count as an AI being, many say a machine must be able to learn and think for itself. As we will see later, there is fast progress toward AIs with not only independent thought, but also qualities such as consciousness, creativity, emotions, and a moral sense too.

High-tech "robots" are used to manufacture and test printed circuit boards used in computers and other consumer electronic devices.

MAKING INTELLIGENT MACHINES

To create a machine that can think, act, and interact in a way that is useful to us is a very complex task. In order to achieve this, scientists working on AI need to understand as much as possible about human thinking and behavior. This is a huge challenge, as there is still a great deal we do not know about how our own minds work. We tend to take for granted many of our abilities:

- incorporating information from our senses to understand the world around us

- moving around as we wish by coordinating our bodies accordingly

- communicating with other people using language

- using seemingly unrelated pieces of information to make sensible decisions

We do not usually think of such skills as indicators of intelligence—they are just part of being human. Not all AIs will need to do every one of these things, but they will need to do some to be practically useful. In order to have any of these complex abilities, they must be programmed with innovative and sophisticated technology.

INDEPENDENT THOUGHT

Traditional computer programs use logic and clear instructions to find

After being defeated by the IBM Watson computer, *Jeopardy* super-champion Ken Jennings (left) added the joking response, "I for one welcome our new computer overlords." Jennings and Brad Rutter (right) were the two most successful Jeopardy contestant in the show's long history. Jennings had won a record 74 matches in a row while Rutter had never lost a Jeopardy match. The televised event in 2011 highlighted the amazing improvements in artificial intelligence over the past few decades.

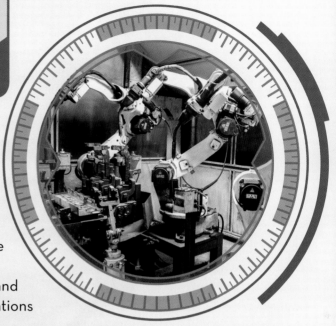

the answer to a question. However, this is not always how people think, and true AI systems must be able to learn so that they can go beyond their original programming. The ability to learn is vital if an AI is to be capable of independent thought.

Humans learn from experience and observation. We compare new situations with past ones, and this helps us to decide how to act. AIs will need to do the same. One important development in AI learning is *artificial neural networks (ANNs)*, computer systems that copy the way the human brain works. They have rules that determine what inputs are required to initiate an action as well as what will make the computer change how it behaves—essentially "learning." ANNs excel at working with speech recognition, computer vision, and tasks that need "thinking." Neural networks are at the heart of AI research.

PROVING INTELLIGENCE

You may have come across *intelligence quotient (IQ)* tests that judge your ability to think quickly and recognize connections between factors. These may only measure certain aspects of intelligence—and they only apply to humans. So how can we prove intelligence in a machine?

Several tests for intelligence in machines have been suggested. One of the most famous is the *Turing test*, named after mathematician Alan Turing. He suggested that a machine could be called intelligent if a person communicating with it—via keyboard and screen—could not tell that it was a machine. There is an annual competition that challenges AI inventions in this way, and the Loebner

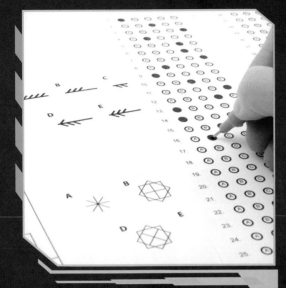

Prize is given for the most human-like chatbot. However, as we have advanced in creating AI systems, many scientists believe that the Turing test is not enough to prove a machine's intelligence—though it is a good start.

IMPLICATIONS OF AI

Why should you worry about progress in AI? Is not real AI too far in the future to even matter? If we consider *Moore's law*—that computer processing power doubles about every 18 months—now is the time to consider the impact of intelligent systems. Progress in all areas of science affects each of us in some way, and AI raises a number of relevant questions.

IQ (intelligence quotient) tests are a way to measure human intelligence through the use of standardized tests.

Many areas of research may hold dangers we know nothing about at the moment. If we make something more intelligent than ourselves, it is not clear if we will be able to control it. We may find that the intelligence of our machines grows more quickly than we had anticipated. What then?

Imagine a world in which there are intelligent machines among us. Will it alter our view of what it is to be human? The way we see ourselves and judge our own intelligence might change if a computer could think, feel, have opinions, and become better at some things than we are. Maybe our idea of the meaning, nature, and value of life will evolve if we can make life, or something very lifelike, out of inanimate materials.

Technological innovations are largely in the hands of the developed world. People working on AI are likely to build systems that reflect the ideas, values, and interests of their own countries—but how AI is developed and used may affect the whole world. People in countries that are not as technologically advanced may not have much say in how AI is used—and even in the countries that are developing AI, many people will be left in the dark. The technology is very complicated, and the questions it raises are difficult. Who will make sure people are told what they need to know in order to make informed choices? Will everyone be able to voice their opions?

We may agree to use AI only for "good" purposes, but people have different ideas of what is "good." Suppose that, after the destruction of the World Trade Center in 2001, the US had been able to use AI systems to destroy terrorist leader Osama bin Laden. Would they have done it? Should they have? Your answer will depend on who and where you are.

We all have a right to be involved in decisions about the world's future. But to have the power to change things, we need to understand the issues that affect us all. You must be able to separate fact from opinion in the things you read and hear, as well as disentangle reliable information from media scare stories and public relations hype. If you can do so and develop your own informed views, you will be able to play an important part in this changing world.

TEXT-DEPENDENT QUESTIONS

1. Name three key developments in the history of AI.

2. Explain the purpose of the Turing test and how it works.

EDUCATIONAL VIDEO

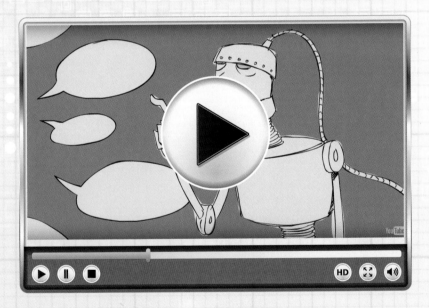

Scan here to watch a video on AI test.

RESEARCH PROJECT

Using the Internet or your school library, research the topic of chatbots, and answer the following question: "Do chatbots lead to better real-life relationships?"

Some say chatbots improve real-life relationships because they help people learn how to have conversations without feeling judged by others. Those who are introverted or shy have opportunities to practice asking and answering questions, leading to confidence in social interactions with people.

Others contend that chatbots are harmful to relationships with other people. Those who are reluctant to call or meet others may depend on chatbots for social interaction and never venture out into the real world. Chatbots are also computer programs that do not have a true sense of humor or the ability to have creative, random conversation that are present between real people.

Write a two-page report, using data you have found in your research to support your conclusion, and present it to your class.

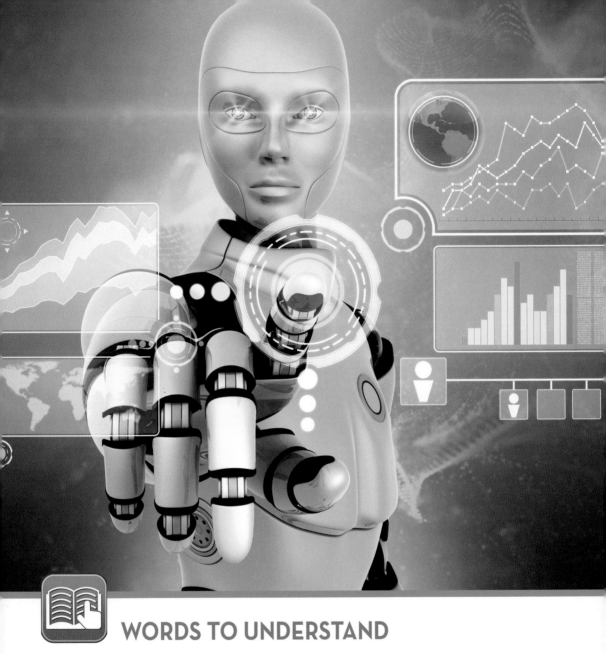

WORDS TO UNDERSTAND

blasphemous—against God or sacred things

consciousness—the state of being awake and able to understand what is happening around you

genome—one set of chromosomes with the genes they contain; the genetic material of an organism

CHAPTER 2

CONSCIOUSNESS AND EMOTIONS IN MACHINES

RENE DESCARTES SAID IN 1637, "I think, therefore I am." Is being alive defined by thinking, learning, and acting? If so, what does this mean about machines that can perform such functions?

Robotic pets have been around for some time now. They are electronic "animals" with simple programming and some sensors and controls, so that they seem to respond when you talk to or play with them. They do not possess AI and cannot learn or make their own choices.

In the future, however, we may see true AI companions for people who need constant care. We might eventually be able to have AI versions of people we love who have passed away. In the film *AI* (2001), a robot child is modeled after the dead son of the director of a robotics company. As AI beings become more and more like humans, will we consider them to have consciousness and emotions? What are the implications?

LIVING MACHINES

It is becoming less clear over time that machines are not alive. We sometimes personify them with phrases such as "My car is dead," or "My alarm clock woke me up."

Robotic pets that can perform certain functions have become popular over the past decade. However, these machines cannot learn from or adapt to their surroundings, unlike real pets.

But whether we can make a truly living machine depends on how we define life. If our machines could think for themselves and work independently without us, could we still say they are not living? We might decide that an AI machine is "alive" in some sense. In such a case, what rights would a thinking, living machine have?

Think about what it means to be alive, and then try to decide whether any alternative forms of life are possible—either things we could make or perhaps beings from another part of the universe. A virus is a very simple organism, yet scientists argue about whether it counts as a living being. Like a human, it has a **genome**, or genetic coding that acts as instructions for its development and functions. We can now make a virus by building it from chemicals strung together in the right order—and an artificial virus behaves in exactly the same way as a naturally occurring one. If we count a virus as a living organism, we can say that we have made artificial life already.

In the novel *Frankenstein* by Mary Shelley, a scientist makes a creature out of parts of dead bodies. The scientist's creation can walk, talk, and act like a living person. The novel raises issues of whether the creature is really alive, and what it means to be a person.

CREATING LIFE

Some people may have religious objections to making something that is intelligent—especially if we cannot agree on whether it is alive. Many people have religious beliefs that say creating life unnaturally is something only God can do, and it is

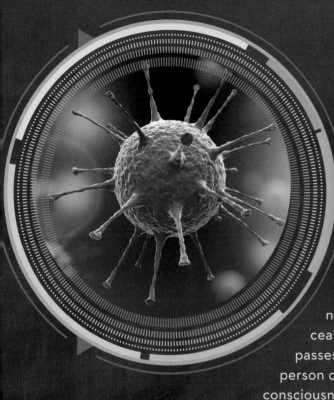

Scientists have created viruses in laboratories—how is this different from the idea of creating an intelligent machine?

blasphemous, or religiously disrespectful, to act like God ourselves and presume that we can create life artificially.

Some people believe that we do not die when our physical bodies cease to work, but our consciousness passes on to a new life, maybe as a person or even another life form. This consciousness might be called a spirit, a soul, or another name. Can an AI being have a spirit?

LIFE AND RIGHTS

Every living person has rights, and in many countries, some animals have rights too. As a person, some of your rights—to food and shelter, for example—are recognized worldwide and confirmed in the United Nations' Universal Declaration of Human Rights. In most countries, national laws protect the rights people have to education, vote in elections, choose who to marry, and so on.

If we build an AI, will it have rights, too? This is a very far-reaching question, and we may decide AIs are entitled to different rights, depending on their type. On one hand, something that can think, is aware of its own existence, and can feel pain or sorrow perhaps should have rights similar to humans'. On the other hand, something that can work out how to make a better bridge but has no feelings maybe should not be given rights.

If we decide that an intelligent machine is a life form, we may have problems

SIDEBAR

AN EMOTIONAL COMPUTER ACTOR

In the film *2001: A Space Odyssey* (1968), an AI computer, HAL, kills three of the spacecraft's crew. Dave, the one crew member left alive, decides to take HAL apart, thereby "killing" him. HAL is aware of this and wants to stay alive: "Dave, stop... Stop, will you? Stop, Dave... Will you stop, Dave...? Stop, Dave. I'm afraid... I'm afraid... I'm afraid, Dave... Dave... my mind is going... I can feel it... I can feel it... My mind is going... There is no question about it. I can feel it... I can feel it... I can feel it... I'm afraid..."

if we want to turn it off. Some may feel it has the right to continue existing—or it may even decide that for itself. To turn it off could be seen as causing "death"—technically, murder. We needto consider what rights any artificial entities will have and what responsibilities we may have toward them.

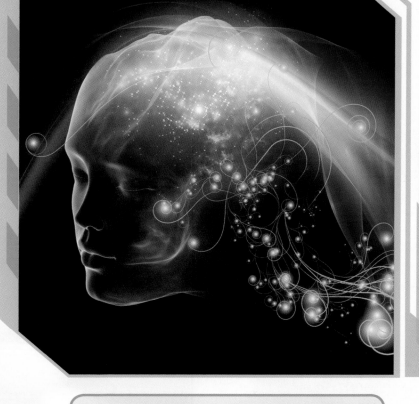

CONSCIOUS MACHINES

Consciousness is the state of being aware of yourself and what is happening around you. There is no consensus on what makes us conscious or where, if anywhere, in our bodies our consciousness lies. We do not know if other creatures have full consciousness like humans, though it seems quite likely that other intelligent animals have some degree of it. Some creatures that work together—like ants and bees—may also have a kind of group consciousness.

Along with artificial intelligence, some scientists are studying whether machines could develop consciousness—awareness of its surroundings and an ability to learn from, and act in response to, outside stimulus.

As we have not yet made a machine that is fully conscious, we do not know how it will behave if we do. We might find it develops consciousness automatically. If this is the case, we will need to decide whether we have any right to limit its ability to think and be aware of itself.

FACING FEELINGS

Our feelings and ability to imagine how other people think and feel help us to work together and get along with other people. If we created living beings without feelings, would we run into trouble?

During the course of each day, you feel many different emotions. You may be happy to get up in the morning or resentful at being woken. You may be excited about, or fearful of, something that you expect to happen. At different points, you may feel disappointed, joyful, angry, ashamed, amused, or pleased—and your feelings affect how you behave. If you forget to feed your pet mouse and it dies, you will perhaps feel sad and guilty. However, if you get another pet mouse, you may be more likely to remember to feed it because of these feelings. If you do

Would artificial emotions help an AI machine to be more effective? For example, a machine developed to recover survivors from an earthquake might try harder to succeed if it felt bad when it didn't find survivors—or proud when it did.

well at something or are kind to someone, you will probably feel good about yourself. This motivates you to continue to do well or show kindness again in the future.

Feelings are important in helping us to function in society, relate to other people, and learn patterns of behavior that are acceptable. If feelings are useful in helping us to learn, would they not also be useful to a learning machine?

EMOTIONS IN AI

The computer systems we have today work in a logical way—they use reason to find answers to problems. But the "reasonable" answer to a problem is not always a workable or acceptable one. Even with an informed understanding of what is unacceptable, an intelligent machine may have difficulty with some of our more inconsistent behaviors. How would it act in life-and-death situations? Consider the following scenario: A person is very sick and in pain, and he will certainly die in a short while. He asks his AI care assistant to kill him. Should the AI do it? Perhaps doing so would be considered merciful—but it may also be cruel and illegal—depending on the person, their family, and their location. Would this matter to an AI assistant?

One of our basic aims in building AIs should be that they do not harm people. However, to teach a machine what would harm people—physically or emotionally— would be difficult. The machine would also need the ability to anticipate how a person might react to something. It may be easier to give the machine feelings itself, letting it have a proper insight into how people think and feel.

Incorporating emotions into AI robots can have multiple benefits to humans. *The Wall Street Journal* reported in 2014 that robots with facial features, voice interaction, and human-like gestures were found to be much preferred over those that did not display such qualities. Emotions make robots more natural for people to interact with, but they may also add efficiency: Two Italian scientists developed robots with emotional circuits in 2010 and found they were better than non-emotional robots at completing programmed tasks such as searching for food, escaping predators, and finding mates. Their conclusion was that emotional states make robots more fit for survival.

While an AI without feelings or understanding of human nature could make dangerous mistakes, a machine with emotions might fall in love, have tantrums, panic, become bored, argue about what it is supposed to do, or just sulk and do nothing! Machines can go wrong, just as people can make mistakes. Imagine a

computer virus that made all AI systems depressed or even harmful. A machine with emotions can be just as dangerous as it may be beneficial.

TALKING WITH AI

When you use a cell phone, you often end up talking to a computer program of some sort. You might leave a message on voicemail, give commands to book tickets, or navigate a menu with voice prompts. As we continue to develop intelligent systems, there may be many more situations in which people interact with machines. Maybe telephone or online help desks could use AI systems to deal with calls—they often have too many calls for their human operators to deal with as it is. Would this work?

A 2013 report by Kleiner, Perkins, Caufield, and Byers indicated there are 2.4 billion Internet users worldwide, and people in the US check their cell phones 150 times per day on average. On both smartphones and the Internet, there are a growing number of interactive AI programs such as Apple's Siri, the Amazon Echo, Google Now, and Microsoft's Cortana. They can verbally answer factual questions posed by a human, play requested music, provide driving directions, buy movie tickets, and even give humorous responses. Such programs make interfacing with a computer seem more like talking to a person, and it is becoming more difficult to tell the difference.

Some people have difficulty accepting that the characters in television soap operas are not real people. They may write to or accost the actors, expecting

SIDEBAR

ELIZA THE COMPUTER THERAPIST

In 1966, a computer system called Eliza was programmed to act like a therapist. It was not an actual AI system—it merely used a simple questioning technique. Eliza responded to people's comments and questions with more questions, much as a human counselor might do to get to the bottom of a person's problems. Eliza did not understand the clients' feedback in any meaningful sense but used keywords to trigger questions that were likely to be suitable. To the surprise of researchers, Eliza was immensely popular.

them to be the characters they play. There could be similar difficulties for some people in recognizing that a voice they talk to on the phone does not belong to a real person but is in fact a computer or AI system. As AIs increasingly resemble humans, this issue will become very difficult as it may not always be possible to tell if the "person" facing you is human at all.

DEEPER CONVERSATIONS

Many people find that talking to a trained counselor or psychotherapist helps them with their problems. This might be a task you think a machine could not possibly do, but recent trials of computerized therapy systems have often had very positive results. People seem to feel that they can keep their dignity intact and preserve their privacy if they talk to a machine instead of a person. We would need to decide what should happen to the information given to an AI therapy program, and what should or could be done with any conclusions the program drew from it. There are strict rules about what a human doctor, therapist, or pastor can do with information given in confidence. We would need similar, and perhaps additional, protection for people confiding in an AI program which could be hacked into.

TEXT-DEPENDENT QUESTIONS

1. What are four functions interactive AI programs can perform at the verbal command of people?

2. Name one positive and one negative factor in using an AI therapist.

EDUCATIONAL VIDEO

Scan here to watch a video on creativity in AI.

RESEARCH PROJECT

Using the Internet or your school library, research the topic of emotions in AI robots, and answer the following question: "Should we strive to build an intelligent robot with emotions?"

Some believe we should seek to incorporate emotions in robots because that would make the robots more aware, responsive, entertaining, and functional, especially as social companions. Research has shown people prefer interacting with machines that display human-like characteristics. The more robots can imitate people, the more possibilities they will have to meet the range of human needs.

Others argue that emotions in robots can lead to disastrous consequences. While some emotions may be beneficial in limited amounts and specific circumstances, too much can cause a robot to be inefficient and difficult to work with. The robot may refuse to follow the orders of a human, or even worse, act in a hostile manner. It may not understand the effects of making life-and-death decisions on people and just make a "calculated" choice. We should focus only on intelligence, not emotions, in AI technology.

Write a two-page report, using data you have found in your research to support your conclusion, and present it to your class.

WORDS TO UNDERSTAND

android—a mobile robot usually with a human form

cybernetics—the scientific study of how people, animals, and machines control and communicate information

cyborg—a person whose body contains mechanical or electrical devices

drone—an unmanned aircraft or ship guided by remote control or onboard computers

prosthesis—an artificial device that replaces a missing or injured part of the body

CHAPTER 3

HOW ARTIFICIAL INTELLIGENCE CAN IMPACT SOCIETY

IN THE PAST, MACHINES REPLACED PEOPLE in repetitive, unskilled tasks such as factory work. However, as AI becomes more sophisticated, it is increasingly able to take on skilled labor and aid in complex work. In the workforce, education, military, and even childcare, AI is showing the potential to be a valuable asset to society.

ANDROIDS AND CYBORGS

It is fairly easy to think of robots as machines as long as they remain visually mechanical. But if we make robots that have a skin-like covering, fur, or other animal attributes—we may find it harder to recognize them as machines. Work is underway not only to build *androids*—robots that look like humans—but also to make a reality of *cyborgs*—humans whose bodies contain mechanical or electrical devices—by giving real people and animals robotic functions.

We all know that it is not just our bodies that make us human. Our minds

Androids, like C3PO from Star Wars, are robots with a human form. So far, androids still have a mechanical look that makes it clear they are not real people.

are really what make us ourselves. So we probably will not demand that an AI looks like us before we accept its intelligence and character. Indeed, researchers have found that people are capable of interacting and forming bonds with even very artificial-looking robots. However, giving a robot some similarity to the human form, such as two "eyes" and an upright stance, helps us to relate to it.

Studies have found that people have an easier time relating to, and interacting with, robots that are humanoid in appearance.

Studies have shown we respond better to robots that have human characteristics, including skin, hair, and body movements. In 2013, scientists at Georgia Tech University developed a robotic skin with thousands of tiny, mechanical hairs that generate electricity when brushed or exposed to pressure. This allows a robot wearing the skin to have a sense of "touch," which could be eventually used in *prostheses*—artificial devices that replace a missing or injured part of the body—or in returning sensation to people who have lost limbs.

In 2016, researchers at the Tokyo Institute of Technology created a robot with a human skeleton and microfilament "muscle" tissues that connect to joints and contract and expand like human muscles. In fact, the robot has the same number of muscles in its leg as people do and can execute smooth movements. However, it is still lacking in strength and needs assistance to walk.

NADINE AND SOPHIA

Combining multiple technologies, robots resembling and interacting like humans have now been developed. Nadine is an android made in 2013 by the Nanyang Technological University in Singapore. With soft skin and flowing brunette hair, Nadine resembles her creator, Professor Nadia Thalmann, as she performs work as a university receptionist. Not only does she greet visitors, smile, make eye contact, and shake hands, but she can even recognize past guests and start conversations based on previous chats. She has her own personality and can express happiness or sadness based on the topic of conversation. Her AI is based on technology similar to Apple's Siri and Microsoft's Cortana, and Thalmann says social robots can address needs for child care, socialization with the elderly, and even health-care services in future.

Professor Nadia Magnenat Thalmann has pioneered research into virtual humans for more than 30 years. Her android Nadine has been called the "World's most human-like robot."

In 2015, Dr. David Hanson of Hanson Robotics created Sophia, an android with lifelike silicon skin that can emulate more than 62 facial expressions. With cameras inside her "eyes" combined with computer algorithms, she is able to "see," follow faces, make eye contact, and recognize individuals. Using tools like Alphabet's

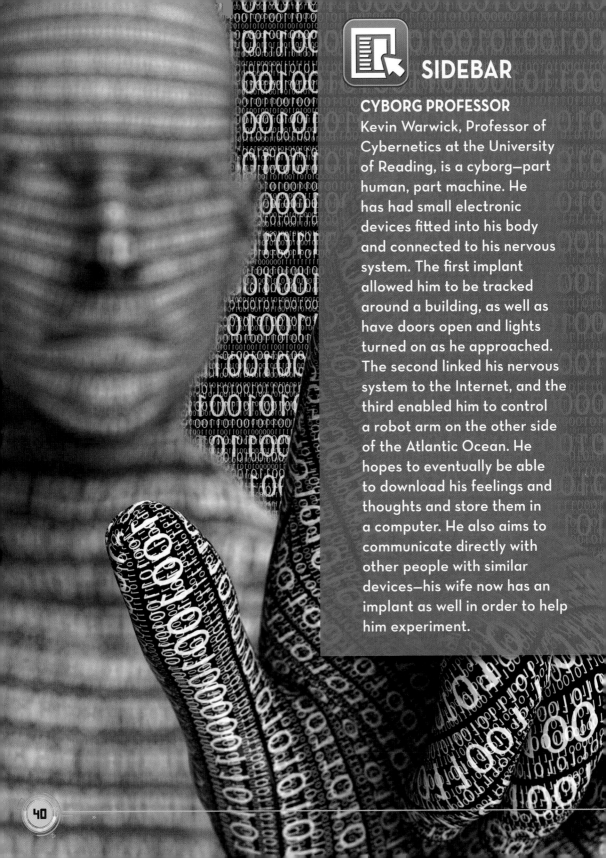

SIDEBAR

CYBORG PROFESSOR

Kevin Warwick, Professor of Cybernetics at the University of Reading, is a cyborg—part human, part machine. He has had small electronic devices fitted into his body and connected to his nervous system. The first implant allowed him to be tracked around a building, as well as have doors open and lights turned on as he approached. The second linked his nervous system to the Internet, and the third enabled him to control a robot arm on the other side of the Atlantic Ocean. He hopes to eventually be able to download his feelings and thoughts and store them in a computer. He also aims to communicate directly with other people with similar devices—his wife now has an implant as well in order to help him experiment.

Google Chrome voice-recognition technology, Sophia can understand speech, speak on topic, and get smarter over time. Hanson said that he believes one day, robots will be indistinguishable from humans, with the ability to walk, play, teach, help, and form real relationships with people. With aging populations and a reduced workforce in many countries, androids like Nadine and Sophia may help to meet practical needs in communities around the world.

CYBERNETICS

Cybernetics is a branch of technology that explores control mechanisms in artificial and biological systems. Scientists in this field are starting to add electronic components to some animals. This is not, at the moment, moving towards creating AI animals, but is going the other way—taking real animals and adapting them with technology to suit our needs.

In Tokyo, researchers have found a way to equip a cockroach with an electronic device that can be remotely controlled to move the insect's legs. The electrical impulse in the legs is the same as it would be if it came from the cockroach's own nervous system, and it causes the cockroach to walk in the direction the controller wants it to go. This technology has also been tested on rats.

If cybernetics were taken to extremes, there is a chance that people could gain "superhuman" abilities by having electronic implants in their brains. They may be able to communicate using telepathy and alleviate pain without drugs. This idea could be used in many areas, from reading the minds of criminal suspects to communicating with people with disabilities who are nonverbal.

AI IN THE WORKFORCE

For every community to function, there are many unpleasant and menial jobs that have to be done. These jobs often fall to people with limited skills or a lack of choice. As we develop AI machines, the goal is usually to serve the needs of people, including doing jobs we do not want to do or cannot do as quickly, cheaply, or efficiently. However, if these jobs are taken by AI beings, how will the people they replaced earn a living?

Many repetitive jobs in factories have already been taken over by machinery. These machines do not require any intelligence, but it could soon be possible for machines to take on expanded roles. These may be the jobs that, although boring, dirty, or unpleasant for a person to do, still need a set of skills that we cannot yet give to a machine. They could include cleaning, fruit picking, and some basic nursing tasks such as emptying bed pans. An intelligent machine may be much more efficient than a person in such work, not needing holidays, breaks, or time off due to illness.

SKILLED LABOR

It is not only unskilled workers who may be replaced by AI systems. As expert systems in areas such as law and medicine improve, they might take over some parts of skilled human jobs. A doctor or lawyer may no longer need such detailed knowledge if they could call on an expert system to support their judgements or diagnoses.

These robots work on an assembly line that produces cars.

Creativity is another area of possibilities for AI. It is already possible to get hold of very basic story-writing programs, and computers can put together simple bits of music. An AI system could try out its compositions on people to see which they like and analyze popular music or literature written by people. If it followed rules and learned with ongoing feedback from humans, it could eventually create popular new entertainment.

AI is already being used effectively in education. Imagine a teacher who knows everything, has superb teaching skills, uses many different approaches to learning to suit your needs—and never gets tired of explaining the same point in different ways. Jill Watson, a virtual teaching assistant (TA) based on

IBM's Watson platform, acted as one of nine TAs in an online course at Georgia Institute of Technology in 2016. She helped answer many of the 10,000 messages from 300 students in online forums, and none of the students knew they were interacting with an AI, as she was answering questions with 97 percent certainty. As technology advances, will an AI program be able to assist in a live classroom? What about important teacher qualities like enthusiasm, care for student progress, and a sense of humor?

In medicine, AI is already being used for diagnosis and treatment. In 2015, IBM acquired Merge Healthcare, which helps doctors store and access medical images. With 30 billion images to "train" its Watson software, IBM is hoping to create AI that can diagnose and treat ailments like cancer and heart disease. Modernizing Medicine is a program that taps the collective knowledge of 3,700 medical providers, 14 million patient visits, and data on how doctors have treated

Robots are now capable of performing surgical techniques that would take medical students years of training to master.

The US military uses robots like the to perform a variety of dangerous tasks, from detonating or defusing land mines and bombs to reconnaissance.

patients with similar profiles. It can instantly mine data and offer treatment recommendations accordingly, which is how the medical community currently makes decisions. AI cannot yet replace doctors at a patient's bedside, but if it eventually can be a physical caregiver, would patients grieve the loss of human interaction or feel relieved someone is not seeing them every day in a fragile state? We would need to assess each person's needs carefully.

One of the most dangerous jobs a person can have is serving as a soldier. What if we could avoid risking human lives in the military? The possible uses of AIs as soldiers or automated weapons are a driving force in getting funding for some areas of research and development.

As of 2013, there were more than 11,000 *drones*—unmanned aircraft or ships guided by remote control or computers—in the US military, but they are almost always remotely piloted rather than autonomous. In 2015, the Pentagon began testing a robot co-pilot that can speak, listen, manipulate flight controls, and read instruments. Like a human co-pilot, it will eventually be able to take off and land a plane, assist on routine flights, and take over flight in emergency situations. It will be visually aware and physically be able to use equipment in the cockpit.

TEXT-DEPENDENT QUESTIONS

1. What is the difference between an android and a cyborg?

2. Name three ways social robots like Nadine and Sophia can potentially benefit a community in the future.

3. Who is Jill Watson, and what is her significance?

4. Describe two ways AI can be used in medicine.

EDUCATIONAL VIDEO

Scan here to watch a video on androids.

RESEARCH PROJECT

Using the Internet or your school library, research the topic of AI in the military, and answer the following question: "Should AI soldiers be used to fight wars?"

Some claim that AI soldiers would be beneficial in wars because there would be fewer human casualties and injuries. Not only would they replace human soldiers who could potentially die, but lives may be saved because they would theoretically not tire, act on emotions, or make mistakes. Drones are an example of carrying out missions with more efficiency and fewer pilots dying.

Others contend that AI soldiers are an extremely dangerous technology. If they are equipped with lethal weapons but cannot understand every situation, there can be grave consequences. AI soldiers may shoot civilians or children, not recognize an enemy who is surrendering, or malfunction and harm whoever is nearby. This could also result in the most technologically advanced army winning, leaving developing countries constantly vulnerable to attack.

Write a two-page report, using data you have found in your research to support your conclusion, and present it to your class.

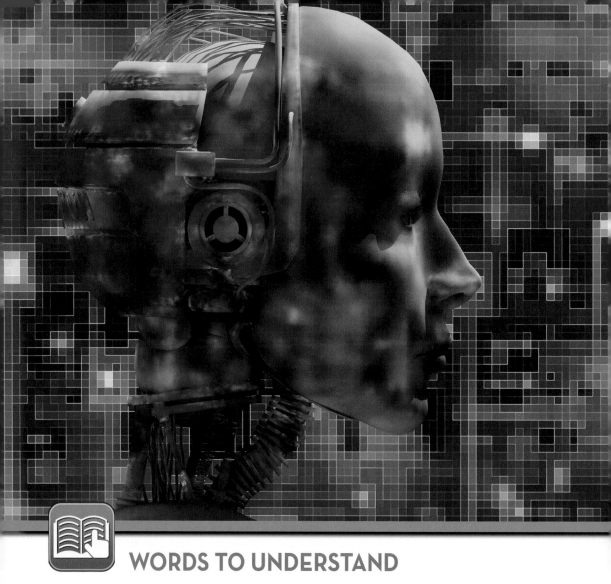

WORDS TO UNDERSTAND

ethical—involving questions of right and wrong behavior

philosopher—a person who studies ideas about knowledge, truth, the nature and meaning of life, etc.

unbiased—not having or showing an unfair tendency to believe that some people, ideas, etc., are better than others; not biased

vested interest—a personal or private reason for wanting something to be done or to happen

CHAPTER 4

ETHICAL ISSUES WITH INTELLIGENT MACHINES

INTELLIGENT SYSTEMS THAT MAKE DECISIONS for us cannot work without guidance about what we consider *ethical*—dealing with right and wrong choices. Whenever we make a decision, we take into account a variety of factors. Many of these are ethical issues, so intelligent systems will need to have a good grasp of these in order to work within human communities.

DEVELOPING A CODE OF ETHICS

Ethics is all about right and wrong. In some cases, many people agree, leading to ethical issues being built into laws. For example, most people agree that we should not kill or take someone else's property, so murder and theft are generally illegal throughout the world. But there is disagreement over some ethical issues. Most vegetarians believe it is wrong to eat animals, for instance, but other people do not have a problem with this. In some cases, there are cultural, religious, or regional differences that influence people's moral stances. In the West, most people believe we should be allowed to marry who we wish, but in many other countries, arranged marriages between strangers are common and even seen as the best system for couples.

Occasionally, we may make exceptions to our beliefs in particular circumstances. Some people—even if they agree that it is wrong to kill—might feel it is acceptable to help someone to die if they are in terrible pain and have asked to die. Others believe the death penalty—executing someone guilty of a serious crime—is necessary to uphold justice, and some countries still enforce capital punishment.

Over time, countries develop systems of what they believe is right and wrong. A code of ethics is not thought up by an individual at one stroke, but they evolve over time with learning and experience by whole populations. Our ideas of morality generally help societies to run smoothly. But where there is disagreement, there may be debate or conflict and, in some cases, war or revolution.

ETHICS FOR MACHINES

Developing a code of ethics in a new field is complicated and often difficult, but we must work to create one if we seek to integrate AI with human life in a healthy manner. Otherwise, an intelligent system will follow its own logic and potentially come up with unacceptable decisions. A human politician would be unlikely to promote saving money on health care by letting seriously ill people die without offering treatment. But a machine trying to make decisions

If you couldn't tell if the voice at a call center was a machine or a person, would it matter?

based on logic and cost efficiency might find this the best course. As we all have different understandings of right and wrong based on our backgrounds and upbringings, it will be difficult to agree on the ethical codes we give to intelligent machines.

Whereas people can be swayed by factors such as public opinion or financial gain, an AI program would apply its ethical code rigorously. An AI equipped with a thorough ethical code would be programmed to follow it—it would not have a choice. However, if machines learn to truly think independently, they may be able to analyze and change the ethical code we give them. For this reason, it would be dangerous to give AI machines "free will" and the ability to ignore their programming. This might happen if someone were to try it as an experiment, if a virus or hacker "broke" an AI system, or if an AI being found programming loopholes that let it reject its guidelines. For these reasons, free will in AIs is a risky proposition—think, for example, of murderers who kill without thinking it is wrong.

RELIGION AND AI

Many ethical codes are closely tied to religious beliefs. In countries such as the US, people are allowed to follow any religion they wish, and the law tries to support them in practicing their faith. In other places, there is one religion that is approved by the state, and all other faiths are banned. Presumably, these countries would want their AI systems to act according to their religious and ethical codes.

If an intelligent computer with information about different religions and beliefs determines that one or another is "right" or "true," there could be very serious consequences for us all. Perhaps an AI being may adopt a religion and reject its original programming. Or it may follow some programmed ethics but not others as it "learns" over time.

It is very difficult for people to make *unbiased* decisions—not influenced by their own feelings, opinions, or interests. In some areas, we may think we are not biased, as everyone we know would make the same choice. But we may be showing a national or cultural bias. Everyone you know may agree that boys and girls have an equal right to education, but this is not held to be true everywhere. A view such as this, built into an AI system, may be accepted in

the West but deemed to be biased, or even an error, if it was applied in some other parts of the world. Any AI will most likely reflect the worldview and ethics of its programmers, who do not all have a uniform set of beliefs.

LEGAL ISSUES

Researchers in AI can generally work freely at the moment, as laws in this field are relatively undeveloped. In 2015, over 1,000 high-profile AI experts and researchers signed an open letter calling for a ban on "offensive autonomous weapons." Among the signatories were Tesla's Elon Musk, Apple co-founder Steve Wozniak, Google DeepMind chief executive Demis Hassabis, and professor Stephen Hawking. They warned of a military AI arms race that could take place in years, not decades, as well as fewer deterrents to going to battle—leading to greater loss of human life. However, this has not yet been translated into law, as legislation cannot always keep up with the fast pace of scientific advances.

Just as there are current arguments regarding topics such as animal rights, genetic engineering, and abortion, countries may disagree about what should and should not be allowed in AI. Still, legal restrictions for each country and for the world are necessary because as AI continues to develop, not all AI use will be conducted for good purposes—there are criminals in every field.

Criminals may use AI for financial or military objectives. We could even see a brand of "AI terrorism" in which terrorists or countries at war use sophisticated programs to change how an AI system acts—drones may be directed to attack their own citizens, defense systems may be shut down by an AI computer, or top secret information could be revealed to the wrong sources. Despite all the benefits AI technology can produce, we cannot be sure that it will not be turned against us. For AI to be useful to us, it must be powerful, but this could also make it dangerous in the wrong hands.

In many areas of technology, new advances have been used for military

purposes and entertainment, and AI may not be any different. It is likely that AI systems—whether robots, androids, or computer software—may be used for violent or sexual intent. How can we prevent AI from being used to threaten people or promote unhealthy sexual behavior?

If someone is harmed by a badly designed item, the designer or manufacturer is liable, or held responsible, and may have to pay compensation to the person who was hurt. If a robot in a car manufacturing factory were to make something faulty, we could hold the designer of the robot or the owner of the car company accountable. But

The Buddhist view that we should live our lives causing as little harm as possible might be a good principle for AIs to follow. But would human nature allow us to program an AI so selflessly?

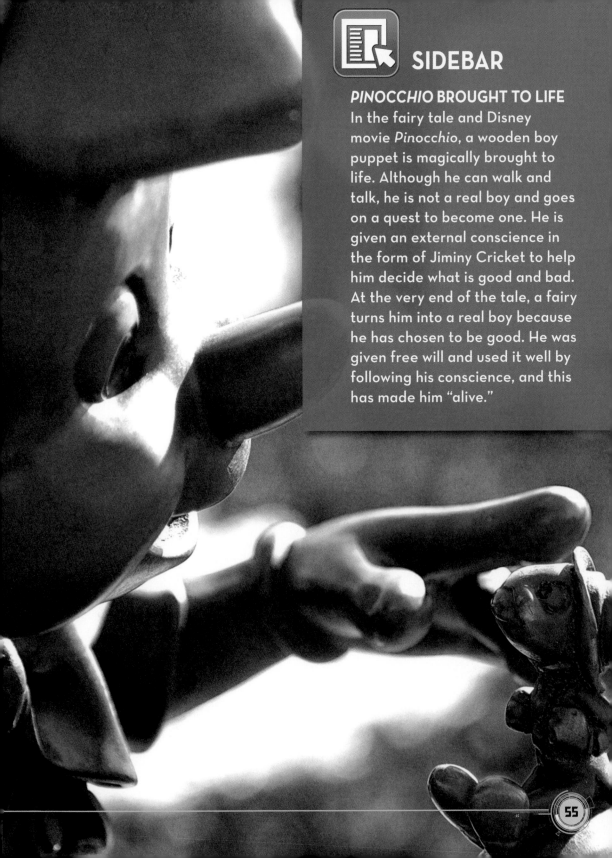

SIDEBAR

PINOCCHIO BROUGHT TO LIFE

In the fairy tale and Disney movie *Pinocchio*, a wooden boy puppet is magically brought to life. Although he can walk and talk, he is not a real boy and goes on a quest to become one. He is given an external conscience in the form of Jiminy Cricket to help him decide what is good and bad. At the very end of the tale, a fairy turns him into a real boy because he has chosen to be good. He was given free will and used it well by following his conscience, and this has made him "alive."

SIDEBAR

COMPUTER STOCKBROKERS

Computers that are used to buy and sell shares on the world's stock markets were partly to blame for the economic crash called "Black Monday" in 1987. The systems were allowed to make their own decisions, and because they worked much faster than people, they quickly sold shares of stock, pushing the prices down. As the prices fell, more computers sold shares, making the prices fall even further. If people had been making the decisions, the fall could have been slower, and people may have been aware of the crash sooner.

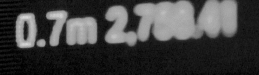

Soldiers set up an AI robot system in the field. Some people are concerned about the possibility of warfare using armed robots.

once we have intelligent systems designing their own devices or making even more intelligent systems, liability becomes more complicated. Any limitations in the design or programming of the first system may lead to more and more errors in future "generations" of AI systems, but the original programmer could place blame on the AI program that is making its own decisions.

ETHICS COMMITTEES

We have seen throughout this book how AI impacts many different aspects of our lives—medicine, social interaction, education, and so on. There are also questions of right and wrong in each of these sectors. Who is monitoring the development of AI and the risks posed to us by new advances?

Ethics committees are groups of people who meet to discuss the work carried out by scientists in research institutions and hospitals. Some of the members are subject experts, and some are *philosophers* with an interest in ethics or morals. Philosophers study ideas about knowledge, truth, and the meaning of life. They may think about issues such as what is right and wrong, how we define intelligence or life, and whether anything other than humans can be conscious beings. This type of understanding is very important to AI development and how we will view the systems we create. Philosophers may be key figures in putting together an ethical code for AIs, but they will not all agree on what it should be.

Beyond debating amongst themselves, they will likely have to dialogue with people who have expertise other arenas, such as economics or politics. An ethics committee tries to represent the views of everyone who will have an interest in an issue and make decisions about what is right and wrong—or what should be allowed and what should not. With a full team assembled, they discuss individual cases as well as more abstract issues.

An ethics committee in a hospital might review the case of an individual patient, or it might be appointed by the government to investigate if research

Some issues provoke heated debate as people try to persuade others of their views. How might we feel about arguing with an AI? Should it be programmed so that it can't change its views?

into a particular area should be permitted. In AI, a committee may study the risks of allowing an intelligent robot to care for a child. Each country may draw up its own laws, and in some areas of research, these can differ considerably.

Many of the people working in controversial fields such as AI have a *vested interest*—they may be trying to make money or further their own careers. But in a specialized area, these people, who may be biased, are the ones who often know most about the issues. How they explain things can make a huge difference to society because our opinions may depend on the information they supply. We need to be sure we are basing our views on relevant facts and not on biased arguments. The more informed we are about AI issues, the more capable we will be in creating balanced guidelines for the areas affected by AI.

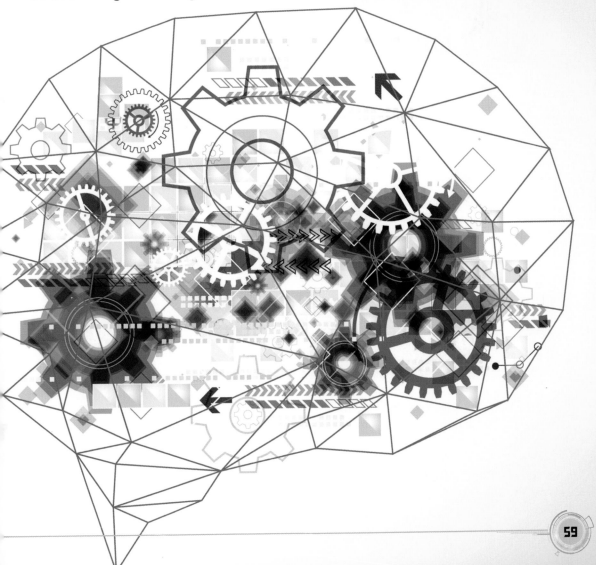

TEXT-DEPENDENT QUESTIONS

1. What are three potential dangers of "AI terrorism"?

2. Who makes up an ethics committee, and what is its purpose?

 EDUCATIONAL VIDEO

Scan here to watch a video on concerns with AI.

RESEARCH PROJECT

Using the Internet or your school library, research the topic of the rights of AI robots, and answer the following question: "Should AI robots be given rights like free will or the ability to physically defend themselves?"

Some contend that AI robots should not be given rights because are not alive naturally. They are created machines that are made to help humans and can be viewed as sophisticated versions of appliances or computers. If they are given free will, they may decide to put themselves above humans and become a danger to people. They may physically fight human attempts to turn them off or change their programming.

Others argue that AI robots are alive if they can act independently, learn, and have positive or negative "emotions." These are qualities of some current robots, and they should be given basic rights, or we will have a new form of slavery where AIs exist solely to follow the commands of people and can be terminated at any point.

Write a two-page report, using data you have found in your research to support your conclusion, and present it to your class.

WORDS TO UNDERSTAND

augment—to make greater, more numerous, larger, or more intense

euthanasia—the act or practice of killing someone who is very sick or injured in order to prevent any more suffering

exoskeleton—an artificial external supporting structure

CHAPTER 5

THE FUTURE OF ARTIFICIAL INTELLIGENCE

HOW MUCH POWER WILL WE GIVE AI machines to make decisions for us? AIs already make important choices to a degree—we let computers decide whether someone is a good candidate for a bank loan, for instance. As more and more decisions are made by computers, our own involvement in running the world may decrease. If we hand over too much responsibility to AI systems, we could end up stranded if they are immobilized by a virus or have a flaw in their programming. Too much reliance on a system that we do not directly control can be dangerous.

On the flip side, AI innovations can be a tremendous boon to humanity. As knowledge about AI is growing, technology is progressing at an increasingly rapid rate. Applications for AI are being developed in more and more areas that can improve the quality of human life. The future of AI is both exciting

The Massachusetts Institute of Technology (MIT) is a leading force in AI development. As well as research labs like this, it has a division looking into the ethics of AI.

and dangerous, and it is important that each generation is informed enough to make wise choices.

AI REPRODUCTION

Computers are very good at tasks that require logic and calculations—they are already better than people at this type of work. This means they can play a valuable role in helping to design other computers. An intelligent computer could be even better than people at building improved AI computers. But could it be that we are only safe as long as the designing and building of AIs stays in human hands? At the moment, we think about the purpose of a new machine and design it accordingly. But computers may come up with very different designs or purposes. Their own "idea" for an improved model or machine may not always match ours.

MIT is already working on ways to get help from computers on designs for intelligent machines. They hope to build design systems that will allow engineers to "chat" with a computer using a whiteboard, drawing sketches and sharing ideas that would normally be done with other people. The computer would ask intelligent questions, make calculations and suggestions, and may soon be able to say how a better computer could be built.

ROBOT REVOLUTION

A world in which computers or robots have taken over the world is common in science fiction books and films. Some people fear we are building a world where this is becoming possible. If we create an AI system that can design other AIs and improve on its

Many books and other forms of entertainment, including the Terminator series of films, have explored the possibilities of a world in which intelligent machines attempt to eradicate humanity.

SIDEBAR

BIG DATA

A human brain automatically categorizes things, but it needs to see many examples before it can distinguish between cats and dogs or Indian and Korean food. The same principle holds true for artificial minds. Even the most advanced computer has to play at least a thousand games of chess before it becomes a formidable opponent. Part of the current AI breakthrough lies in the massive amount of collected data about our world, called big data, which provides the information that AIs need. If you search for a necklace online, the websites you visit after that may have advertisements for necklaces. That is big data at work, learning what types of products you are interested in. Huge databases, self-tracking, web cookies, online footprints, years and years of search results, and the entire digital universe are at the disposal of AIs to learn from.

own abilities, it may begin to wonder about the role of people in the world. War, famine, cruelty, and destruction of the environment are evils that an AI may want to end. Following logic alone, AIs could decide that people have done a poor job of managing the planet and that machines could do better. It might seem impossible to think that intelligent machines could ever take control from people. Is this just a nightmare scenario, or could it be a real threat?

Researchers into AI are divided over this question. Some argue that we are safe because we control the power and manufacture of the machines—we can cut their power supply or stop building them, for instance. Others say that as AI programs communicate using the Internet, they will be able to control the power networks and may be smart enough to avoid our attempts at stopping them. We are so dependent on computer-controlled systems that we could well be held hostage by machines that could, for example, detonate bombs, immobilize the police, or cause economic disasters.

POTENTIAL AI INNOVATIONS

Though there are ample risks involved in expanding the capability and reach of AI, there is also an equal potential for AI to

Google has been working to develop self-driving vehicle technology for more than a decade. By the start of 2017, the company's self-driving car prototypes had driven more than 1.7 million miles. Google hopes to have the technology available to the public as early as 2020.

benefit people. AI may be the key to solutions to problems we have yet to figure out and give people abilities that were only imagined.

One constant goal of developing AI is to prolong or save human lives. AI can be used to take care of the elderly and allow for independence much longer into life. This would free family members of seniors to continue working and perhaps simultaneously reduce medical costs in a country. As cars become increasingly able to drive themselves and adapt to new environments, AI may eliminate traffic accidents altogether.

The ways AI can be used to *augment*, or increase, human abilities is another area of exciting research. Cyborgs may not just be science-

AI technology could one day help improve prosthetic devices for people who have lost limbs.

fiction concepts, but integrating technology into human bodies can be a real possibility for many. How much more productive would we be if we added AI devices that could work with our brains, giving us perfect memories or the ability to do complex mathematical calculations? What if we could access the Internet with our brains and download skills like typing or language acquisition? If someone loses a limb, AI could be created to know how to control a robotic limb, enabling efficient swimming and fine motor movements. Along that line, an intelligent *exoskeleton* can help the elderly walk effortlessly well into old age.

As robots become more intelligent and integrate emotions, they may be able to have seamless conversations with humans. This can change social interactions, as people may gravitate toward AI friends instead of pets or human

Many factory workers were replaced by automated systems in the 20th century. What will happen as the 21st century progresses?

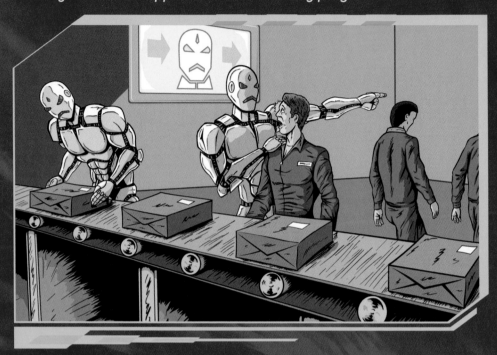

relationships. From child care to companionship for seniors, intelligent systems may revolutionize how we define friendship, family, and community.

CONSEQUENCES TO ADVANCEMENT

With the new frontier of AI innovations, impactful consequences will follow, and we must consider how to address these concerns. If AI technology can make cyborgs a reality, with augmented human abilities, these opportunities would likely be available only to the extremely rich. This could widen the gap between the rich and poor even further if the poor cannot afford brain implants or bionic limbs.

Will intelligent, social robots vastly reduce the quantity and quality of human-to-human relationships? If people can interact with robotic beings that are more agreeable and straightforward, will they still choose to befriend humans who might be moody and argumentative? Simple things like texting and social media alone have affected how much people have face-to-face interactions and live phone conversations. AI technology can fundamentally change how people approach relationships and community—for better or worse.

If AI systems take over both menial and skilled jobs, what will become of the unemployed humans they replace? The rise of unemployment in the US in past years has often been coupled with poor mental health and higher crime rates. Yet entire sectors of jobs could be taken over by robots. The effect can trickle down to education, as it can become less rewarding to go to college or beyond if someone incurs debt but has fewer job opportunities. Will people then become devalued because they have less to contribute to society? If so, what how would laws on abortion or *euthanasia*—intentionally ending another person's life to prevent suffering—be affected?

MOVING FORWARD

AI robots may be indistinguishable from humans in the next couple of decades. They could be engineered to think, learn, feel, and act as independent beings with unlimited capabilities for knowledge and efficiency. Like developments in biology and chemistry—which have led to brand new medicines but also dangers such as chemical warfare—AI has tremendous potential and risk.

People must anticipate the challenges to come as technology quickly improves. Ethical committees need thoughtful members to write healthy, moral codes of ethics. Government officials, judges, and lawyers have to work together to make appropriate laws in the AI sector. Leaders in the military need to set limits on how much intelligent systems can do in war. And people in each of these areas must communicate across sectors with each other to maximize the benefits of AI technology while minimizing the harm. The more people learn and dialogue about AI, the better chance we have of informed decisions as we move forward.

TEXT-DEPENDENT QUESTIONS

1. What are four potential AI innovations that can benefit society?

2. Name three possible negative consequences to be careful about if AI advances in the future.

 EDUCATIONAL VIDEO

Scan here to watch a video on future possibilities of AI.

RESEARCH PROJECT

Using the Internet or your school library, research the topic of social AI, and answer the following question: "Would social relationships with AI robots be positive for humans?"

Some believe that relationships with AIs would be beneficial because AIs would always be available, cooperative, and oriented to help people. Positive relationships would be modeled and make people more cooperative with one another. People without human companions would not be left alone and be happier if they could live with an AI robot. People could still choose to meet other people, so AIs do not necessarily stop human relationships.

Others maintain that human interaction cannot ever truly be replaced because robots cannot have the same sense of humor, creativity, randomness, and genuine love that people are capable of. For this reason, people who depend on AIs for social needs may never be completely fulfilled. Also, without the potential for disagreement from robots, bad ideas may not be challenged, and people would not learn how to deal with conflict in a healthy manner. They may be used to a master-servant relationship and shy away from human interactions based on equality.

Write a two-page report, using data you have found in your research to support your conclusion, and present it to your class.

SERIES GLOSSARY OF KEY TERMS

anomaly—something that differs from the expectations generated by an established scientific idea. Anomalous observations may inspire scientists to reconsider, modify, or come up with alternatives to an accepted theory or hypothesis.

evidence—test results and/or observations that may either help support or help refute a scientific idea. In general, raw data are considered evidence only once they have been interpreted in a way that reflects on the accuracy of a scientific idea.

experiment—a scientific test that involves manipulating some factor or factors in a system in order to see how those changes affect the outcome or behavior of the system.

hypothesis—a proposed explanation for a fairly narrow set of phenomena, usually
based on prior experience, scientific background knowledge, preliminary observations, and logic.

natural world—all the components of the physical universe, as well as the natural forces at work on those things.

objective—to consider and represent facts without being influenced by biases, opinions, or emotions. Scientists strive to be objective, not subjective, in their reasoning about scientific issues.

observe—to note, record, or attend to a result, occurrence, or phenomenon.

science—knowledge of the natural world, as well as the process through which that knowledge is built through testing ideas with evidence gathered from the natural world.

subjective—referring to something that is influenced by biases, opinions, and/or emotions. Scientists strive to be objective, not subjective, in their reasoning about scientific issues.

test—an observation or experiment that could provide evidence regarding the accuracy of a scientific idea. Testing involves figuring out what one would expect to observe if an idea were correct and comparing that expectation to what one actually observes.

theory—a broad, natural explanation for a wide range of phenomena in science. Theories are concise, coherent, systematic, predictive, and broadly applicable, often integrating and generalizing many hypotheses. Theories accepted by the scientific community are generally strongly supported by many different lines of evidence. However, theories may be modified or overturned as new evidence is discovered.

FURTHER READING

Barrat, James. *Our Final Invention: Artificial Intelligence and the End of the Human Era.* New York: St. Martin's Press, 2015.

Bostrom, Nick. *Superintelligence: Paths, Dangers, Strategies.* Oxford: Oxford University Press, 2016.

Chace, Calum. *Surviving AI: The promise and peril of artificial intelligence.* San Mateo, CA: Three C's Publishing, 2015.

Del Monte, Louis A. *The Artificial Intelligence Revolution: Will Artificial Intelligence Serve Us Or Replace Us?* USA: Louis A. Del Monte, 2014.

George, Binto. *Artificial Intelligence Simplified: Understanding Basic Concepts.* Bettendorf, IA: CSTrends LLP, 2016.

Kaplan, Jerry. *Humans Need Not Apply: A Guide to Wealth and Work in the Age of Artificial Intelligence.* New Haven, CT: Yale University Press, 2015.

Kelly, John E., III. *Smart Machines: IBM's Watson and the Era of Cognitive Computing.* New York: Columbia University Press, 2013.

INTERNET RESOURCES

http://aitopics.org/
AITopics is a collection of information about the research, people, and applications of AI. Its mission is to educate and inspire through a wide variety of organized resources gathered from across the web, including articles, videos, podcasts, and book references.

http://www.csail.mit.edu/
The Computer Science and Artificial Intelligence Laboratory (CSAIL) is the largest research laboratory at MIT and one of the world's most important centers of information technology research. They seek to understand intelligence in living systems, build artificial systems capable of intelligent reasoning, perception, and behavior, and build principled models of reasoning and thinking applicable to a wide variety of real-world problems. The website includes the latest news, research, and resources in AI.

http://www.mitsuku.com/
Mitsuku is a chatbot that won the Leobner Prize in AI for chatbots in 2013. Mitsuku answers questions posed by humans by showing related images and gathering information from related websites.

https://www.sciencedaily.com/news/computers_math/artificial_intelligence/
Science Daily provides the latest news articles and videos on technology topics, including AI. The website provides summaries for each article as well as the full text.

http://spectrum.ieee.org/robotics/artificial-intelligence
IEEE Spectrum is the online magazine of the world's largest professional organization devoted to engineering and the applied sciences. It provides information about major trends and developments in technology, engineering, and science—including AI—with blogs, podcasts, news, and feature stories, videos, and interactive infographics.

INDEX

Numbers in ***bold italics*** refer to captions.

ABOUT THE AUTHOR

Dave Bond is a freelance writer who lives in Hackensack, New Jersey. A graduate of Rutgers University, he has written numerous articles and essays on scientific and engineering topics. He also wrote the book *Genetic Engineering* in this series.

PUBLISHER'S NOTE

The websites that are cited in this book were active at the time of publication. The publisher is not responsible for websites that have changed their address or discontinued operation since the date of publication. The publisher reviews and updates websites each time this book is reprinted.

PHOTO CREDITS